POP PIANO HITS

SIMPLE ARRANGEMENTS FOR STUDENTS OF ALL AGES

City of Stars, Mercy & More Hot Singles

Contents

2 **CITY OF STARS** .... *from LA LA Land*

16 **EVERMORE** .... *from BEAUTY AND THE BEAST*

7 **MERCY** .... *Shawn Mendes*

22 **PERFECT** .... *Ed Sheeran*

28 **STAY** .... *Zedd and Alessia Cara*

ISBN 978-1-4950-9574-0

7777 W. BLUEMOUND RD. P.O. BOX 13819 MILWAUKEE, WI 53213

Visit Hal Leonard Online at
www.halleonard.com

CITY OF STARS
from LA LA LAND

Music by JUSTIN HURWITZ
Lyrics by BENJ PASEK & JUSTIN PAUL

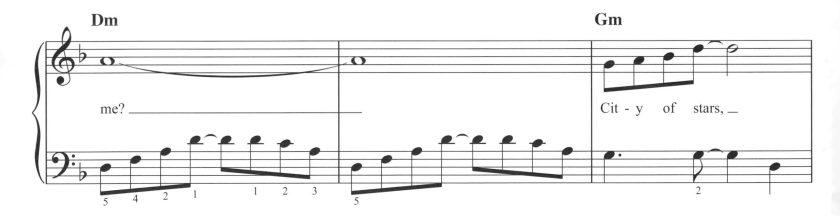

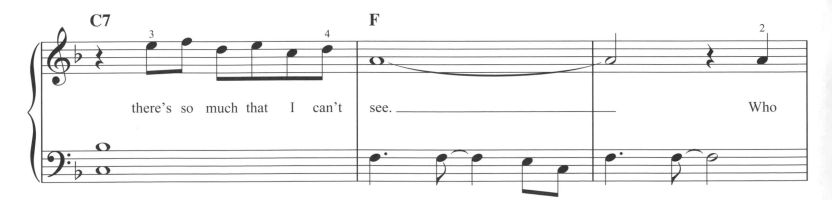

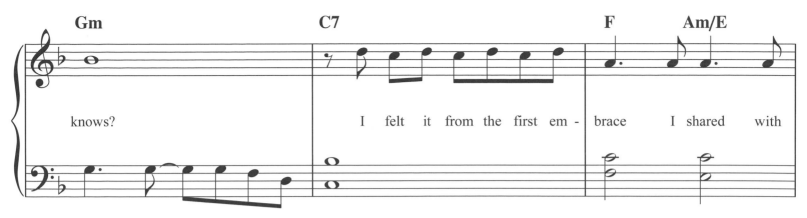

Gm   **C7**   **F**   **Am/E**

knows?   I felt it from the first em - brace I shared with

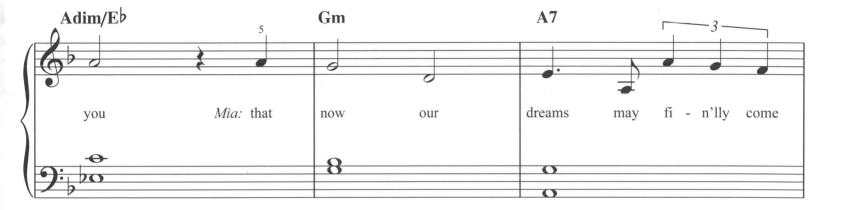

Adim/E♭   **Gm**   **A7**

you   *Mia:* that   now   our   dreams   may   fi - n'lly   come

Dm   **Gm**

true.   Cit - y   of   stars, ___

C7   **Dm**

just one thing ev -'ry - bod - y   wants,

there in the bars ___ and through the smoke-screen of the crowd - ed res - tau - rants: ___

___ it's love. Yes, all we're look - ing for is

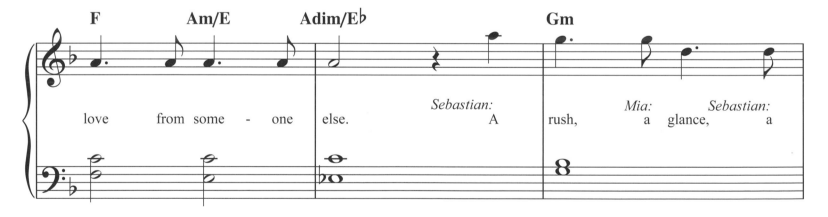

love from some - one else.

Sebastian: A rush, *Mia:* a glance, *Sebastian:* a

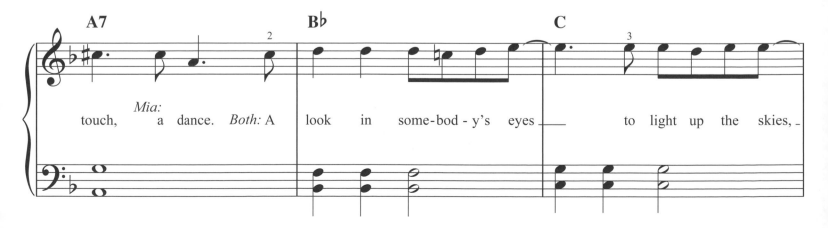

touch, *Mia:* a dance. *Both:* A look in some-bod - y's eyes ___ to light up the skies, ___

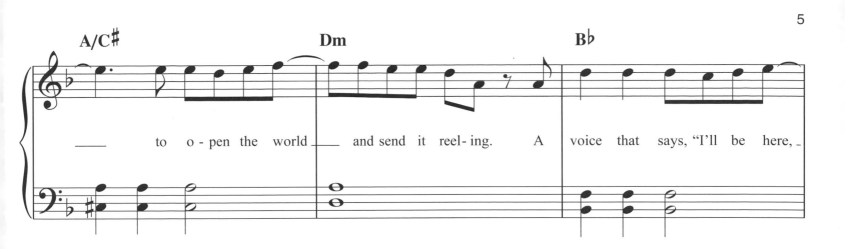

to o - pen the world ___ and send it reel - ing. A voice that says, "I'll be here, ___

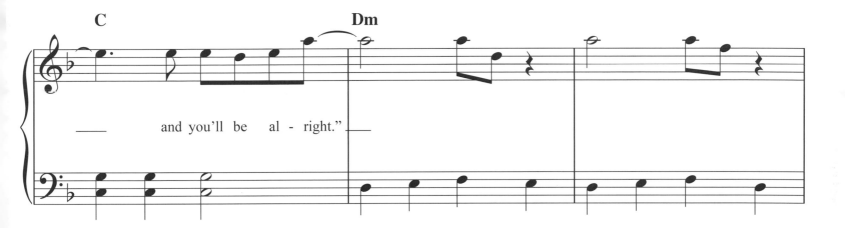

___ and you'll be al - right." ___

I don't care if I know ___ just where I will go, ___ 'cause all that I need's ___

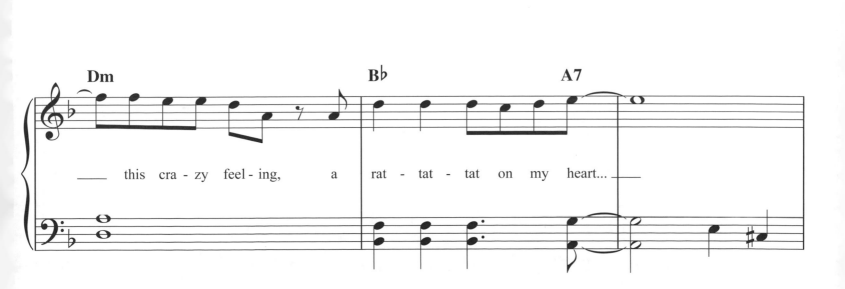

___ this cra - zy feel - ing, a rat - tat - tat on my heart... ___

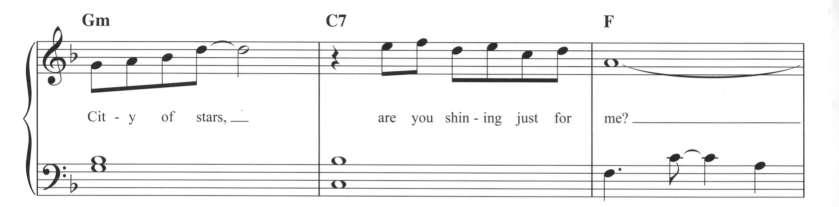

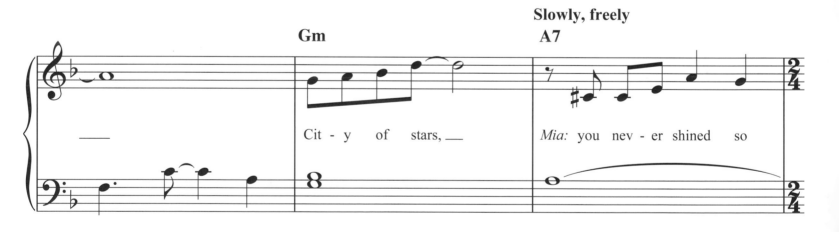

MERCY

Words and Music by SHAWN MENDES,
TEDDY GEIGER, DANNY PARKER
and ILSEY JUBER

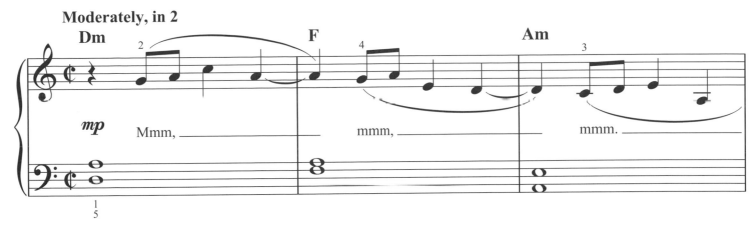

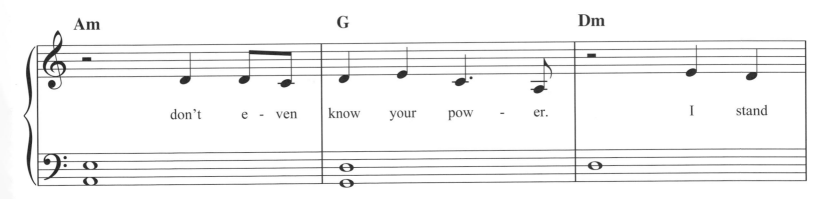

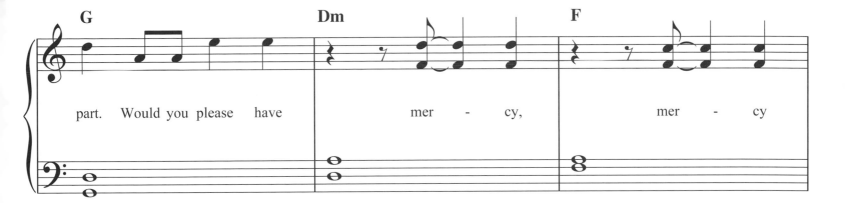

I'd drive _____ through the night just to be

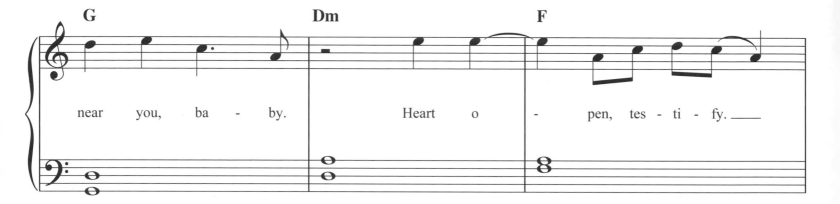

near you, ba - by. Heart o - pen, tes - ti - fy. _____

Tell me that I'm not cra - zy. I'm not _____ ask -

- in' for a lot, just that you're hon - est with me. _____

And my ___ pride is all I got. I'm say - in',

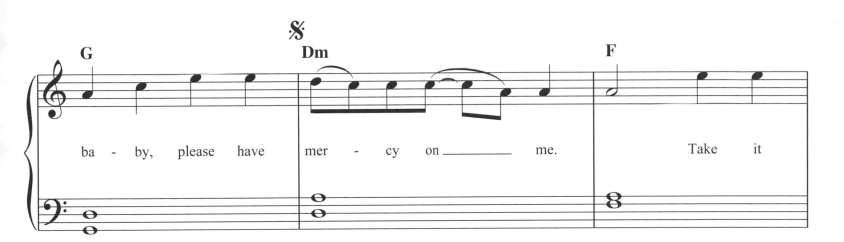

ba - by, please have mer - cy on ___ me. Take it

eas - y on ___ my heart. E - ven though you don't mean ___ to hurt ___ me,

you keep tear - in' me ___ a - part. Would you please have

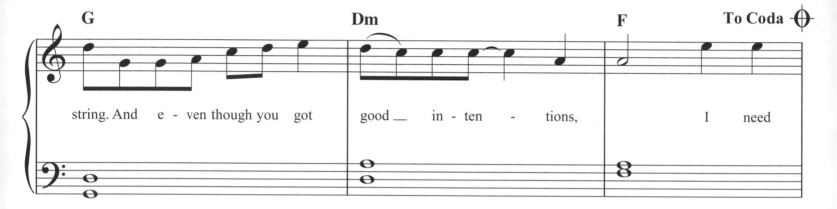

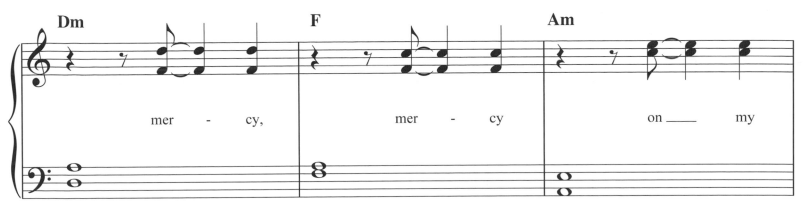

mer - cy, mer - cy on ____ my

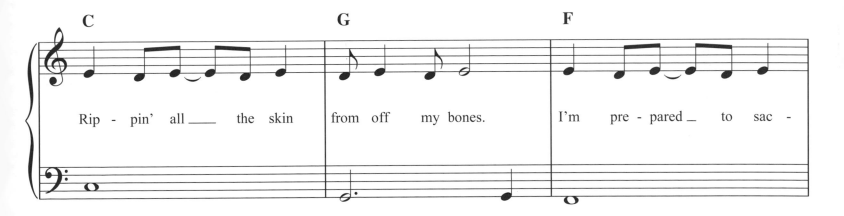

heart? Con - sum - in' all ____ the air in - side my lungs.

Rip - pin' all ____ the skin from off my bones. I'm pre - pared __ to sac -

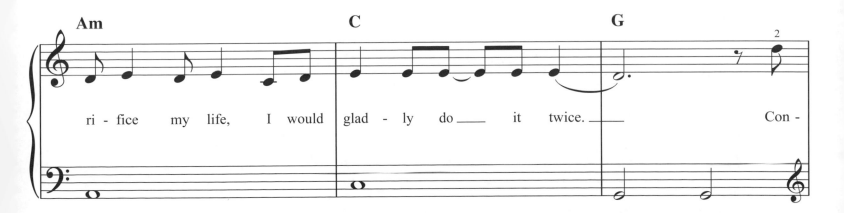

ri - fice my life, I would glad - ly do ____ it twice. ____ Con -

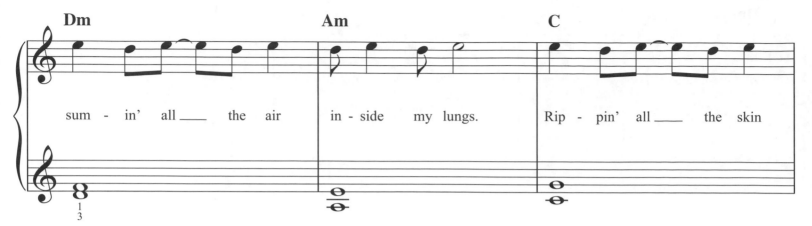

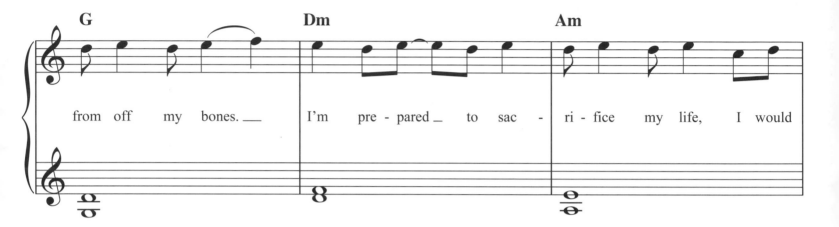

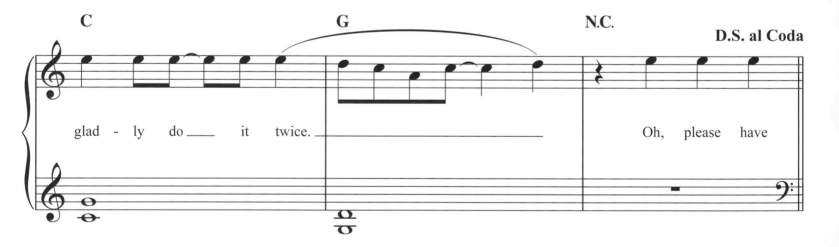

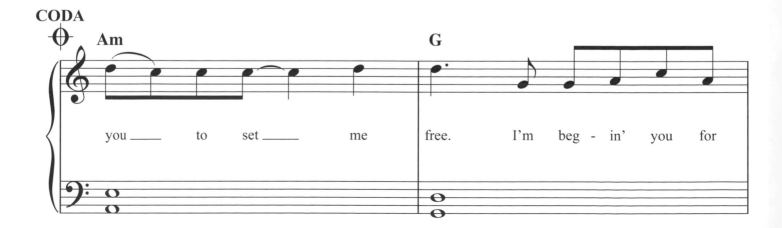

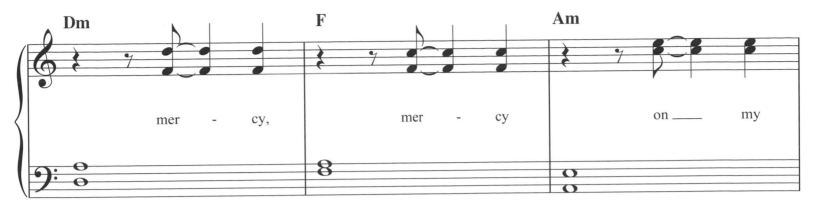

mer - cy,   mer - cy   on ____ my

heart.   I'm beg - gin' you for   mer - cy,   mer - cy

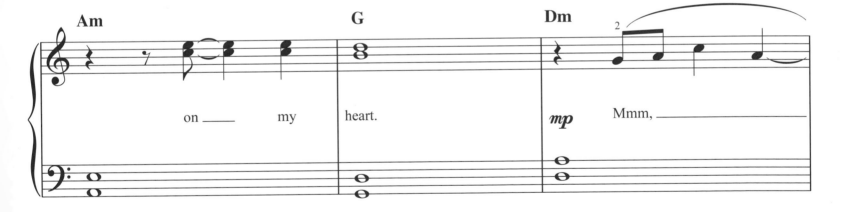

on ____ my   heart.   *mp*   Mmm, ____

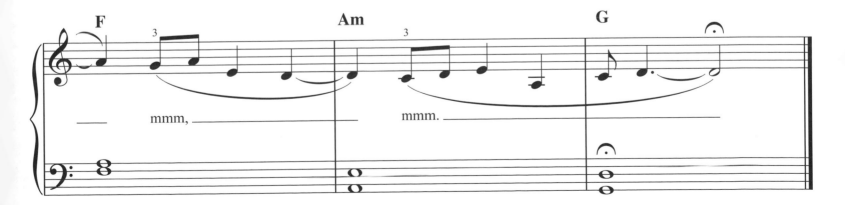

____ mmm, ____   mmm.

EVERMORE
from BEAUTY AND THE BEAST

Music by ALAN MENKEN
Lyrics by TIM RICE

Moderately slow, with freedom

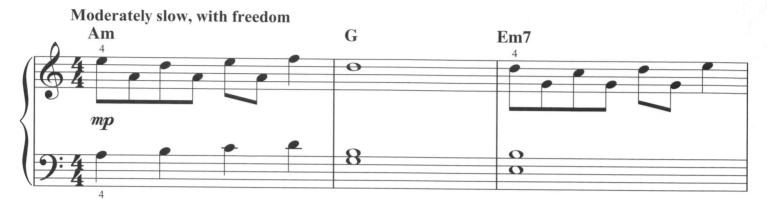

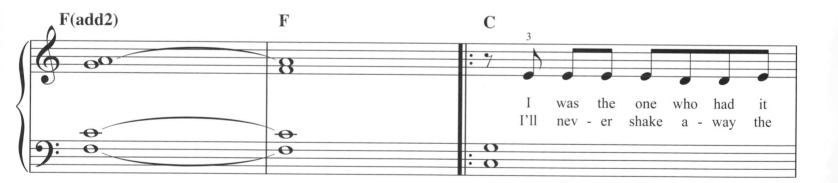

I was the one who had it
I'll nev - er shake a - way the

all;   I was the mas - ter of my
pain.   I close my eyes, but she's still

fate.
there.

I nev-er need-ed an-y-bod-y in my life;
I let her steal in-to my mel-an-chol-y heart;

I learned the truth too late.
it's more than I can bear. _____

Now I know she'll nev - er leave me, e - ven

as she runs a - way. She will still tor - ment ___ me,

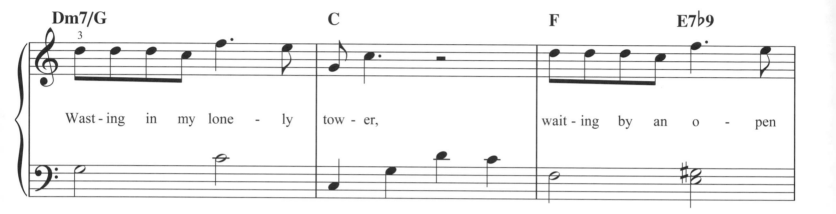

I rage a-gainst the trials of love. I curse the fad-ing of the

light. Though she's al-read-y flown so far be-yond my reach,

she's nev-er out of sight. Now I

know she'll nev-er leave me, e-ven as she fades from

view. She will still in - spire me, be a part ___ of

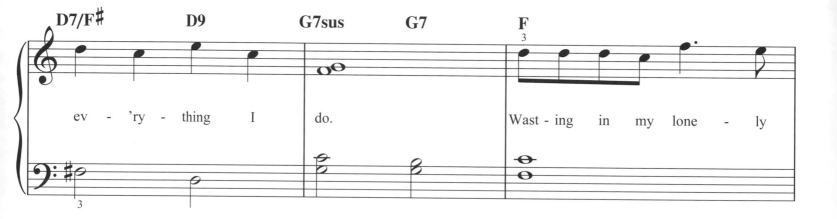

ev - 'ry - thing I do. Wast - ing in my lone - ly

tow - er, wait - ing by an o - pen door,

I'll fool my - self she'll walk right in,

and as the long, long nights be - gin,

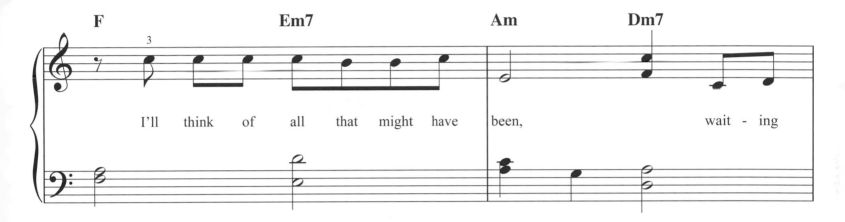

I'll think of all that might have been, wait - ing

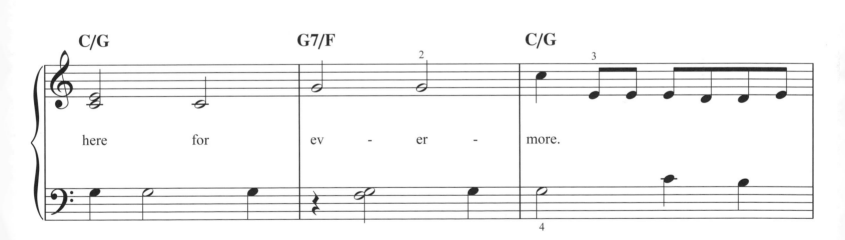

here for ev - er - more.

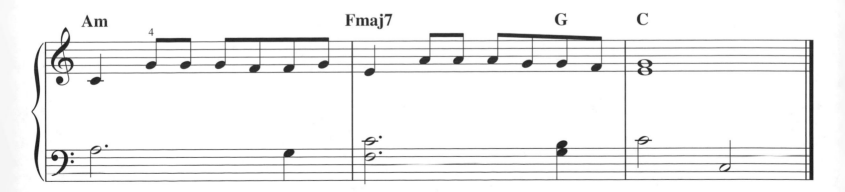

PERFECT

Words and Music by
ED SHEERAN

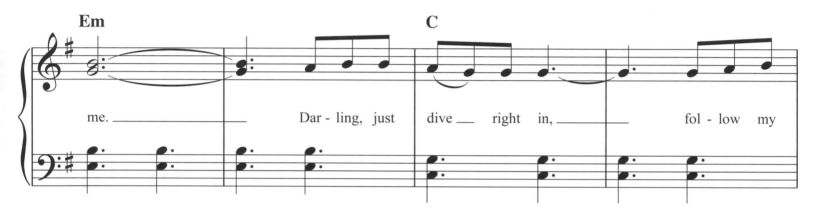

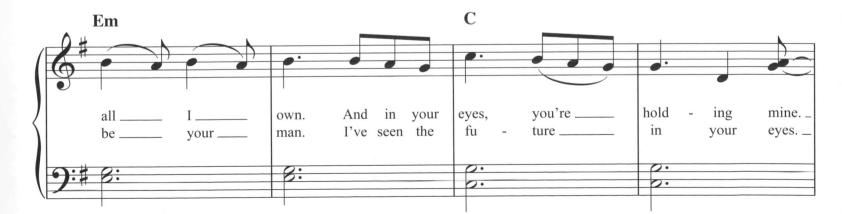

24

Ba - by, _____ I'm dancing in the

dark _____ with you be-tween my arms. Bare - foot on the

grass, lis - ten - ing to our fa - v'rite song. {When you said you looked a / When I saw you in that

mess, I whis-pered un - der-neath my breath. But you heard it, dar - ling,
dress, look - ing so beau - ti - ful. I don't ___ de - serve this, dar - ling,

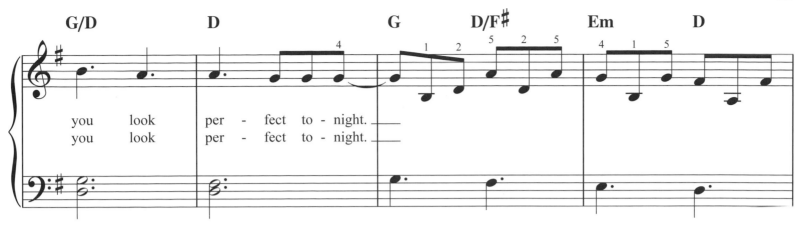

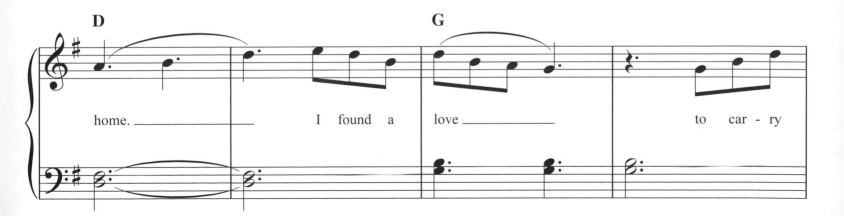

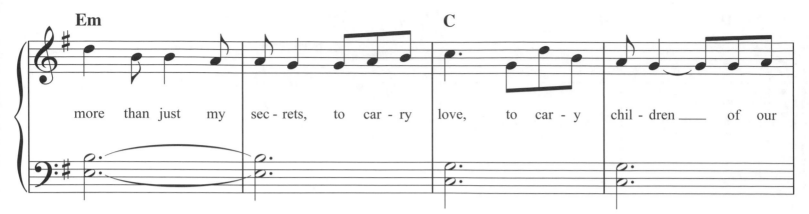

more than just my sec - rets, to car - ry love, to car - y chil - dren _____ of our

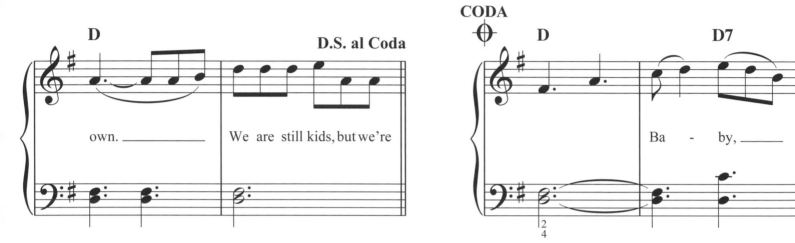

own. _____ We are still kids, but we're

CODA

Ba - by, _____

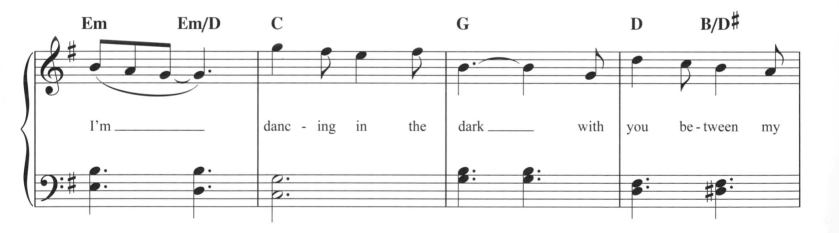

I'm _____ danc - ing in the dark _____ with you be - tween my

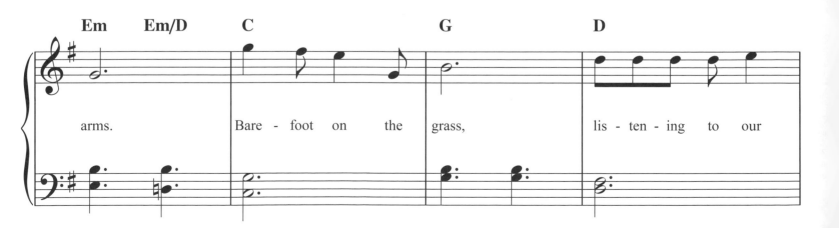

arms. Bare - foot on the grass, lis - ten - ing to our

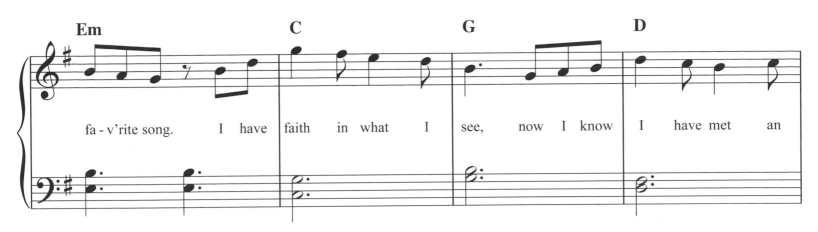

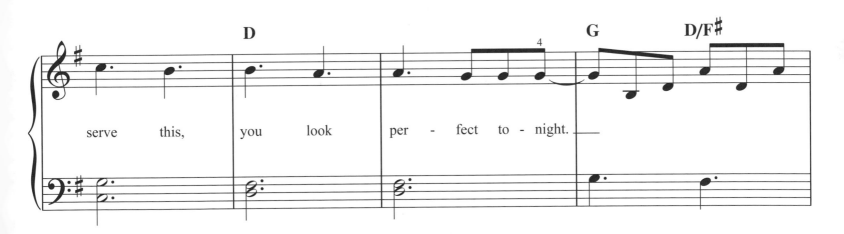

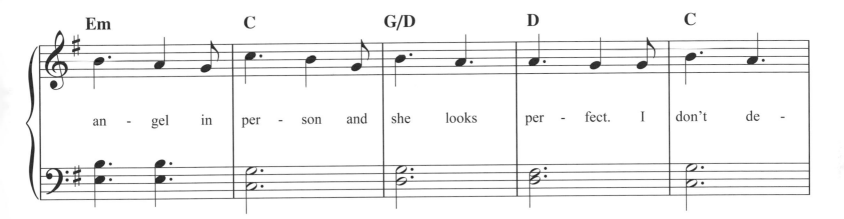

STAY

Words and Music by ALESSIA CARACCIOLO,
ANDERS FROEN, JONNALI PARMENIUS,
SARAH AARONS, ANTON ZASLAVSKI
and LINUS WIKLUND

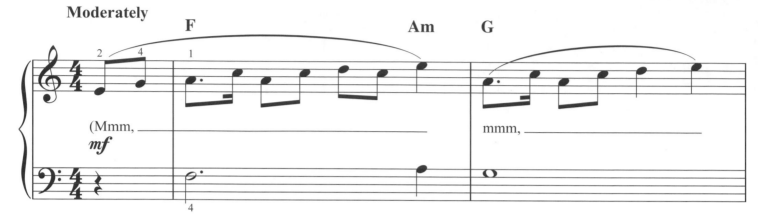

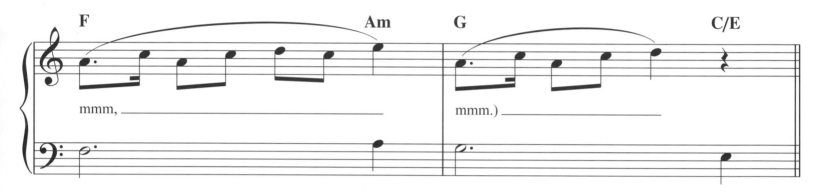

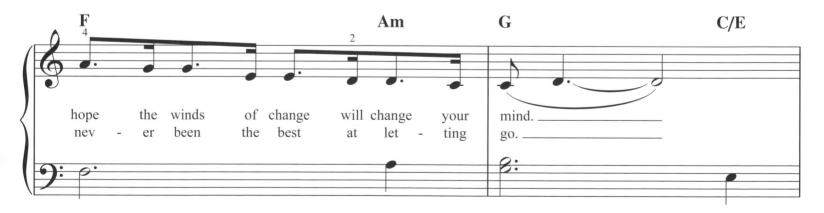

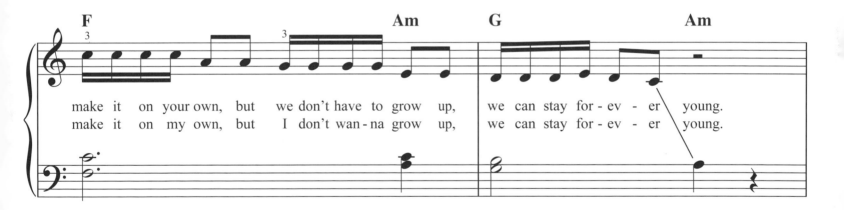

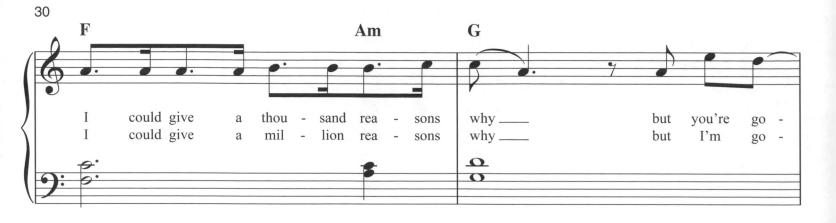

I could give a thou - sand rea - sons why ____ but you're go -
I could give a mil - lion rea - sons why ____ but I'm go -

- ing, and you know ____ that.
- ing, and you know ____ that.

All you have to do is

stay ____ a min - ute, just take your time, the clock is tick - ing, so

stay. ____ All you have to do is wait a sec - ond, your

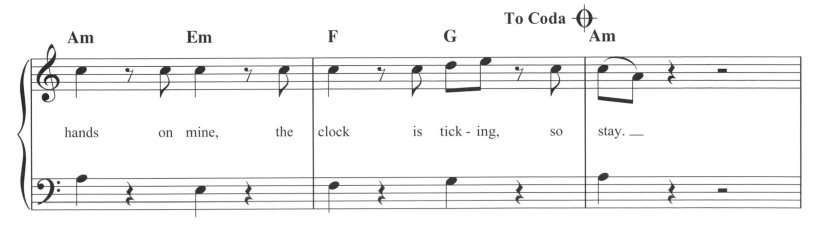

hands   on mine,   the   clock   is   tick - ing,   so   stay. __

All you have to do is...

All you have to do is stay. __   stay. __

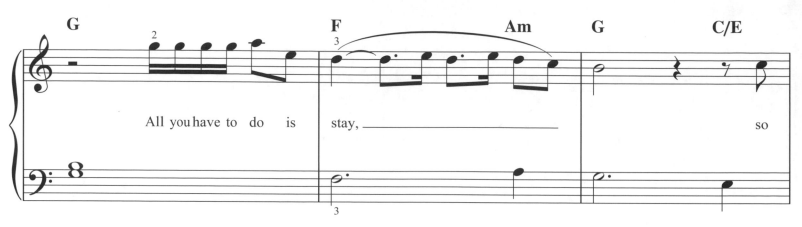

All you have to do is stay, _____ so

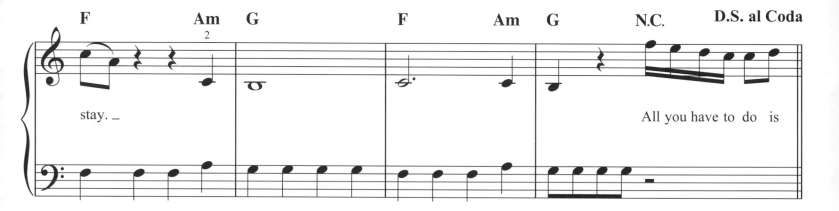

stay. _ stay. All you have to do is

D.S. al Coda

CODA

stay. __ All you have to do is stay. __ (Mmm, _____

mmm, _____ mmm, _____ mmm.) _____